Living in Balance

Anna Baker

Index

Anna Baker

Anna Baker

The Power of Inner Balance

The power of inner balance is a topic that seems simple, but in practice it turns out to be a challenge for many people. We live in a world that constantly pushes us to extremes. We are told that we must be the best at work, be successful in our relationships, always be busy and productive. At the same time, we hear about the importance of inner peace and tranquility. So, we find ourselves in a paradox: on the one hand, society demands that we always be better, and on the other hand, our emotional well-being asks us to stop and find calm. This is the starting point to understand why it is essential to find inner balance in our lives.

Inner balance isn't about being happy all the time or living a problem-free life. Rather, it refers to the ability to maintain a sense of stability, even when chaos surrounds us. Imagine a tightrope. Walking it requires concentration, careful stepping, and the ability to maintain balance, even when strong winds blow. The same goes for our emotions and thoughts. Life often tests us, with moments of stress, sadness, or anxiety, but if we manage to find that inner balance, we can continue moving forward without falling.

To achieve this balance, the first step is to learn to know ourselves. Everyone has different ways of reacting to stress or adversity. Some people get angry easily, others withdraw and prefer not to face their problems, while others try to distract themselves without really resolving what is affecting them. Self-knowledge is key because, by understanding our natural responses, we can begin to work on changing those that destabilize us. This process may be uncomfortable at first, because facing oneself is not always easy, but it is a necessary step to build a solid inner balance.

In addition to knowing ourselves, it is crucial to practice acceptance. Often, we wish things were different than they are. We want problems to go away, difficult situations to not exist, but the reality is that life will always have ups and downs. By accepting that not everything is under our control, we begin to release the weight of frustration. This acceptance does not mean giving up or stopping trying to improve, but rather understanding that there are times when we must simply flow with what happens. This mindset helps us stay calm, even when things are not going the way we expect.

Another fundamental tool for inner balance is the management of emotions. Emotions are not our enemies; in fact, they are important signals that tell us how we feel about life situations. However, we often let them dominate our minds. Anger, sadness or fear can take control if we do not learn to manage them properly. To achieve this management, it is necessary to learn to recognize when an emotion is beginning to affect our inner peace. A useful technique is conscious breathing. When we feel that an emotion is overwhelming us, stopping for a few seconds, breathing deeply and observing what we are feeling can make the difference between reacting impulsively or responding in a balanced way.

Inner balance also has a lot to do with how we manage our thoughts. We all have an inner voice that speaks to us constantly. Sometimes it encourages us, but other times it can be very critical. It's easy to fall into a spiral of negative thoughts that make us feel insecure, anxious or sad. To prevent these thoughts from throwing us off balance, it's important to learn to observe them without letting them get the better of us.

Imagine that your thoughts are like clouds in the sky. Some are light and white, others are dark and heavy, but they all pass eventually. Instead of holding on to negative thoughts, we can let them pass without them affecting our peace of mind.

Inner balance is not something that is achieved overnight, it is an ongoing process. Some days we will feel more balanced than others, and that is okay. The important thing is to have the tools necessary to bring us back to center when we feel that we are going off track. These tools can be meditation, breathing, physical exercise, or simply taking a few minutes a day to reflect. There is no one way to achieve inner balance, as each person is different, but the essential thing is to find what works for you and make it part of your daily routine.

Finally, it is important to remember that having an inner balance does not mean avoiding life's challenges. On the contrary, it is a way of facing them with greater strength and serenity. Life will always present us with obstacles, but if we have cultivated that inner balance, we will be able to face them more effectively, without losing our calm or mental clarity. Living in balance is an act of self-care and self-love, because it allows us to be more aware of our needs and limits, and at the same time, to be more present for others.

A Balance in All Areas

A balance in all areas of life is, in essence, a goal that many people wish to achieve, but which often seems difficult to achieve. However, it is important to understand that it is not about having everything under control or having every aspect of our life perfect. It is rather about making sure that we are paying attention to the key parts of our existence in a way that allows us to feel at peace and satisfied with who we are and what we have. The different areas of life, such as health, work, relationships, personal growth and leisure, are all connected to each other. If one of them is out of balance, it can affect the others, so the goal is to learn to maintain a harmony that allows us to be in tune with ourselves.

One of the most important areas we need to balance is health. And we're not just talking about physical health, which is vital, but also emotional and mental health. The body and mind work together, so if we're constantly stressed, anxious or depressed, our body will feel it too. Likewise, if we don't take care of our diet, if we don't exercise or if we don't get enough sleep, it's likely that our mind will also be affected. That's why it's crucial that we start to see our health as a fundamental piece of that balance. Eating well, moving regularly, getting enough sleep and taking care of our emotional well-being are aspects that, although they may seem simple, have a profound impact on how we feel on a daily basis.

Another key aspect is work. For many, work consumes a large part of their time and energy, and that's okay, as long as it doesn't become the only priority. It's common for people to focus so much on their careers that they forget about the other areas of life, such as personal relationships or time for themselves. Work is necessary, and for some, it can be a source of personal satisfaction, but it's important not to let work be the only thing that defines our life. If we allow work to consume us completely, we're likely to end up exhausted and, worse, dissatisfied, because when we neglect the other areas of our life, sooner or later we'll feel the emptiness of what we've left behind.

Personal relationships are another key pillar of balance. Our connections with others, whether family, friends or partners, play a big role in how we feel about our lives. However, it's easy to fall into relationships that throw us off balance, either because they demand too much of us or because they don't give us the support we need. Balance in relationships involves setting clear boundaries, knowing when to say no and making sure the people we spend time with are helping us grow and not stagnate. It's also about understanding that relationships should be reciprocal: it's not just about giving or receiving, but about a balance between the two. When our relationships are healthy and balanced, we feel happier, calmer and more connected to the world.

Personal growth is also an essential part of life balance. Sometimes, we may feel like we are stuck in a rut or not making progress toward our goals. It is at these times that we need to pay attention to our personal development. Learning new things, whether about ourselves or the world, is a powerful way to stay motivated and balanced. Personal growth doesn't always have to be something grandiose; it can be as simple as reading a book, taking a class, pursuing a new hobby, or reflecting on our goals and how we can achieve them. The point is to keep growing and evolving, because when we feel stuck, the imbalance starts to manifest itself in other areas of our life.

Leisure, on the other hand, is a part of the balance that we often ignore. In a world that values productivity and achievement so highly, leisure time may seem like a luxury or even a waste of time, but it is actually essential for our well-being. Leisure does not simply mean doing nothing, but rather spending time on activities that relax us, entertain us or allow us to disconnect from daily stress. This can be anything from spending time with friends, to going for a walk, playing a sport or simply enjoying a good book. Leisure time allows us to recharge our batteries and return to our daily activities with a clearer mind and a renewed spirit.

Financial balance is also an area that cannot be ignored. It is not about having great wealth, but rather about managing money in a way that does not cause us constant stress or anxiety. Money is a tool, not an end in itself, and learning to use it wisely is key to preventing it from becoming a source of imbalance. Financial peace of mind is achieved when we are aware of our income and expenses, when we plan for the future without sacrificing the present, and when we avoid comparing ourselves to others. Finding this financial balance gives us a sense of security that contributes to our overall well-being.

Finally, balance in all areas of life is not something that can be achieved all at once, nor is it a permanent state. There will be times when one area will require more attention than another, and that is normal. The important thing is to be aware of when one part of our life begins to become unbalanced and to take steps to correct the course before it affects the rest of our areas. Balance is a dynamic process, and the more aware we are of how the different areas of our life interact, the easier it will be to maintain that harmony that allows us to feel fulfilled and at peace.

The First Step Towards Balance

The first step towards balance in life is self-knowledge. This means that in order to achieve a balanced life, we must first know ourselves. It may seem like a basic thing, but in reality many people live their lives without stopping to think about who they really are or what they want. We get used to following the expectations of others, doing what we are supposed to do, without asking ourselves if that makes us happy or if it is what we really want. Self-knowledge is the key to begin to balance our lives, because it allows us to identify which areas need more attention and which ones are working well. It is like taking a personal inventory, where we review our emotions, thoughts, habits and behaviors to better understand how we are handling ourselves in life.

An easy way to start getting to know ourselves better is to ask ourselves questions. What makes me happy? What stresses me out? What are my long-term goals? Am I satisfied with my life right now? These questions help us see more clearly what aspects of our lives are out of balance. Sometimes it can be hard to admit that something isn't right, but we need to be honest with ourselves. If we don't, it's like we're driving a car without knowing where we're going. We can move forward, but we'll likely end up somewhere we didn't want to be. Self-knowledge gives us the map we need to steer in the right direction.

In addition to asking ourselves questions, another powerful tool for getting to know ourselves better is reflection. Everyday life is fast-paced and full of distractions. Between work, family responsibilities, and social media, we often don't have a moment to stop and think about ourselves. But reflection is essential to understanding what's going on inside us. Taking a few minutes a day to be quiet, without distractions, allows us to hear our emotions and thoughts in a clearer way. Through reflection, we can identify patterns in our behavior that help us see why we react a certain way in certain situations. Maybe we realize that we always feel stressed when we're around certain people, or that we tend to avoid situations that make us feel uncomfortable. These observations provide us with valuable insights into what we need to change or adjust to achieve greater balance.

The next step in the process of self-knowledge is to accept who we are, with our strengths and weaknesses. Often, when we get to know ourselves better, we can discover aspects of ourselves that we don't like. Maybe we are more impatient than we thought, or maybe we realize that we have a hard time saying no to others. Instead of punishing ourselves for these characteristics, it is important to accept them as part of who we are. We all have areas in which we can improve, and that is precisely the purpose of getting to know ourselves better: identifying where we need to make adjustments. Accepting ourselves as we are does not mean that we cannot change or improve, but it is an essential first step to begin working on our personal balance.

Self-awareness also helps us identify our priorities. Often, imbalance in our lives is because we are devoting too much time and energy to things that are not really important to us. Maybe we are working too many hours at a job that does not satisfy us, or maybe we are spending our energy trying to please other people. When we know ourselves better, we can begin to question whether these decisions are aligned with our true desires and values. By identifying our priorities, we can begin to make changes that will bring us closer to a more balanced life. For example, if we find that what we value most is spending time with our family, but our work keeps us away, we might begin to look for ways to better balance our work responsibilities with our family relationships.

Self-awareness also helps us understand our emotions. Often, we get carried away by emotions like stress, anger, or sadness, without really stopping to think about where they come from or why we feel the way we do. When we take the time to get to know ourselves better, we can begin to identify the triggers for our emotions and how we react to them. This allows us to develop greater emotional awareness, which is crucial to maintaining balance in our lives. Instead of automatically reacting to our emotions, we can learn to manage them more effectively. For example, if we know that traffic makes us grumpy, we can find ways to calm our mind before we face it, such as listening to relaxing music or practicing deep breathing techniques.

Finally, self-awareness helps us to be more compassionate with ourselves. We live in a society that puts pressure on us to be perfect at all times. We are expected to be successful at work, to have perfect relationships, to always be happy and in control. But the reality is that we are all human, and part of being human is making mistakes and facing difficulties. When we know ourselves better, we also learn to be more understanding of ourselves in the moments when things don't go the way we expected. Instead of punishing or criticizing ourselves, we can see those situations as opportunities to learn and grow.

The first step towards balance, then, is a process of internal exploration. It is not about reaching a point of perfection, but about understanding ourselves better and accepting who we are. In doing so, we can begin to make more conscious decisions that are aligned with what we really want in life, and that will allow us to move towards greater peace and stability. Over time, as we continue with this process of self-knowledge, we can adjust our lives so that each of our actions better reflects our values and needs, leading us to a more balanced and fulfilling life.

Anna Baker

Managing Ups and Downs

Handling the ups and downs in life is a crucial skill for maintaining balance. Life, by its nature, is full of ups and downs. There are days when everything seems to be going our way, when we feel like the world is on our side and things are flowing smoothly. But there are also days when it seems like everything is against us, when stress, anxiety, or hardship overwhelms us. Coping with these moments of ups and downs is part of the human experience, but what really makes the difference is how we handle those fluctuations. Maintaining balance, even when external circumstances are constantly changing, is possible if we learn to effectively manage these emotional peaks and difficult situations.

The first step to handling ups and downs is to accept that they are inevitable. Many of us fall into the trap of thinking that life should be constant, that if we work hard enough, are positive enough, or do things "right," we can avoid difficult times. The reality is that no matter how prepared we are or how well we plan our lives, there will always be factors outside of our control that will cause us to go through difficult times. Acceptance is key, because instead of resisting or trying to avoid difficulties, we learn to flow with them. By accepting that life has ups and downs, we also reduce the amount of stress we feel when things don't go our way.

One of the most useful tools for handling ups and downs is developing resilience. Resilience is the ability to adapt and bounce back from difficult times. It doesn't mean we don't feel pain or sadness when things get tough, but it does mean we have the strength to keep going despite those emotions. Resilience isn't something we're born with; it's a skill we can develop over time. The key to developing resilience is learning to view challenges as opportunities for growth rather than insurmountable obstacles. When faced with a difficult situation, we can ask ourselves: What can I learn from this? How can I come out stronger? These questions change our perspective and allow us to face life's downs with a more positive and constructive mindset.

Another essential tool for managing highs and lows is emotional regulation. Emotions, such as stress, sadness, or frustration, are normal and human, but if we don't manage them properly, they can take over and throw us off balance.

Learning to recognize our emotions and finding healthy ways to manage them is critical. For example, when we're going through an emotional low, instead of letting ourselves get carried away by despair, we can take a moment to breathe deeply, talk to someone we trust, or journal about what we're feeling. These actions help us process our emotions effectively, instead of letting them drag us into a state of imbalance. Similarly, when we're on an emotional high, it's important to keep our feet on the ground. Euphoria is wonderful, but if we get too carried away by it, we can make impulsive decisions or ignore important aspects of our life that require our attention.

Balance is not only about staying calm during the downs, but also about learning to enjoy and take advantage of the ups. Often, when we are in a positive stage of life, we focus so much on enjoying the moment that we forget to plan or take care of other important aspects. It is like being on top of a mountain, where the view is spectacular, but we also need to make sure that we do not get dizzy from the altitude. Taking advantage of the ups in life means being grateful for the good times, enjoying what we have, but not losing sight of the bigger picture. It is important to continue taking care of our health, our relationships and our responsibilities, even when things are going well.

An essential part of handling ups and downs is keeping a long-term perspective. When we're in a down moment, it's easy to feel like the moment will last forever, but the reality is that emotions and situations are always changing. Nothing is permanent. The same goes for ups: While we enjoy the good times, we must also remember that things will eventually change. Keeping a balanced perspective helps us not get overwhelmed by the tough times or get too carried away by the good times. By remembering that everything is temporary, we can face the ups and downs with more serenity and mental clarity.

Self-care also plays a key role in managing the ups and downs. When we're going through a tough time, it's easy to forget about ourselves and neglect our basic needs. But self-care is what helps us recharge and stay strong, both physically and emotionally. Getting a good night's sleep, eating a balanced diet, exercising, and taking time to relax are key aspects that help us cope better with difficulties. Likewise, when we're in a positive time, self-care allows us to maintain that balance, preventing us from burning out or exhausting ourselves by trying to do too much in too little time.

Another important aspect of managing ups and downs is social support. We don't have to go through life's ups and downs alone. Surrounding ourselves with people who support us, listen to us, and understand us is essential to maintaining balance. Talking to friends, family, or even seeking professional support, such as a therapist, can be a big help when we're going through a difficult time. Sometimes just sharing what we're feeling with someone else brings relief and allows us to see things from a new perspective. Likewise, during times of ups, sharing our joys with others helps us enjoy those good times more and strengthen our relationships.

Ultimately, handling ups and downs is about being flexible and adaptable. Life is not linear, and the sooner we accept that things don't always go the way we expect, the easier it will be to find our footing. Flexibility allows us to adapt to changes and unexpected circumstances without losing our center. This means being willing to change plans when necessary, adjust our expectations, and keep moving forward, even when things don't turn out the way we thought. Instead of resisting changes, we can learn to flow with them, knowing that both ups and downs are part of a natural cycle that always moves forward.

In short, managing life's ups and downs requires a combination of acceptance, resilience, emotional regulation, long-term perspective, self-care, social support, and flexibility. If we can develop these skills, we can maintain balance throughout life's inevitable ups and downs, and face any challenge with greater serenity and inner strength.

Strategies for a Clear Mind

Having a clear mind is one of the fundamental pillars to achieving a balanced life. Without mental clarity, it is easy to feel overwhelmed, confused or disoriented, which can affect our ability to make decisions, solve problems and live fully. The accelerated pace of modern life, responsibilities, stress and constant distractions can cloud our minds and make us feel as if we are trapped in a whirlwind of disorganized thoughts. That is why it is important to develop strategies that help us clear our minds and keep them clear. This will allow us to face challenges with greater calm and wisdom, make better decisions and ultimately live with more inner peace.

One of the most effective strategies for having a clear mind is the practice of meditation. Meditation doesn't have to be complicated or require you to sit in silence for hours. Even just a few minutes a day can make a big difference. Meditation involves focusing your attention on the present moment, letting go of worries about the past or future. When we meditate, we train our mind to become calm and focused, which helps us clear away the thoughts that overwhelm us. Over time, regular meditation practice not only improves our ability to concentrate, but it also reduces stress and anxiety levels, creating a clearer, more orderly mental space. If you've never tried meditating, you can start with simple exercises, such as focusing on your breathing or the sounds around you.

Another important strategy for clearing your mind is to keep your surroundings organized. While it may seem like mental clarity has little to do with physical order, the reality is that our surroundings can greatly influence how we feel mentally. When we're surrounded by clutter, our minds can feel like they're in a constant state of chaos, which creates stress and makes it difficult to concentrate. On the other hand, when our space is clean and organized, it's easier to feel like we have control over our thoughts as well. Taking time to organize our workspace or home can be a first step toward creating an environment that supports a clearer mind. It's not about having everything perfect, but about creating a space that allows us to feel calmer and less overwhelmed.

Time management also plays a key role in mental clarity. When we have a lot of tasks on our plate and don't know where to start, our minds can become filled with anxiety, preventing us from thinking clearly. To avoid this, it's helpful to adopt time management strategies, such as making to-do lists or setting priorities. When we break down our responsibilities into more manageable tasks, we feel less overwhelmed and more able to focus on what really matters. It's also important to learn to say no to commitments that aren't essential. Often, our minds will become clouded if we're constantly overloaded with too many responsibilities. By learning to manage our time more efficiently, we can create a clearer, more focused mental space.

Physical exercise is another powerful tool for achieving a clear mind. When we move, we release physical and mental tensions that build up throughout the day. You don't need to do an intense workout; even a 20-minute walk can be enough to clear your mind and reduce stress. Exercise not only improves physical health, but it also helps release endorphins, which are feel-good hormones. This contributes to improving our mood and calming the mind. Plus, simply stepping away from our tasks and doing something that engages our body allows us to disconnect from the thoughts that overwhelm us and return to our activities with a fresher, clearer perspective.

Diet also directly influences our mental clarity. What we eat affects our brain and our ability to focus. Foods high in sugar or saturated fat can make us feel sluggish and heavy, which affects our ability to think clearly. Instead, a balanced diet rich in fruits, vegetables, whole grains, and lean proteins can improve our focus and mental energy. Staying hydrated is equally important; dehydration can cause fatigue and brain fog, which prevents us from having a clear mind. Therefore, paying attention to what we eat and drink can have a significant impact on our ability to maintain a clear and alert mind.

Adequate rest is another key strategy for achieving mental clarity. When we don't get enough sleep, our brains don't function optimally. Lack of sleep affects our memory, focus, and ability to make decisions. That's why it's crucial to make sure we get the sleep we need every night. Creating a sleep routine that includes regular bedtimes and wake-up times can help improve the quality of our rest. Additionally, it's helpful to avoid using screens before bed, as the blue light emitted by electronic devices can interfere with the production of melatonin, a hormone that regulates sleep. When we get enough rest, our minds are clearer, more alert, and better prepared to face the challenges of the day.

Another helpful strategy for a clear mind is learning to let go of what we can't control. Often, our minds will become clouded when we're trying to solve problems or worry about things that are out of our control. We stress about the weather, other people's actions, or situations we can't change. When we put mental energy into these things, we simply drain our ability to focus and be clear. So one of the keys to keeping a clear mind is to accept that there are things we can't change, and stop worrying about them. Instead, we can focus our energy on what is within our control, which allows us to feel a greater sense of peace and clarity.

Practicing gratitude can also be a powerful tool for clearing your mind. When you are grateful for what you have, your mind is less likely to be filled with negative thoughts or unnecessary worries. Spending a few minutes each day reflecting on the things you are grateful for can help you maintain a more positive and clear mindset. Gratitude helps you focus on the present and appreciate the little things around you, which in turn reduces mental noise and allows you to think more clearly.

Finally, it's important to limit the time we spend on activities that overwhelm our minds, such as excessive use of social media or constant consumption of negative news. These activities can fill our minds with unnecessary information, leading to confusion and anxiety. Setting limits on the time we spend on these activities can be a great way to protect our mental clarity. Instead of spending hours surfing the internet or watching the news, we can spend time on activities that truly nourish us, such as reading, chatting with friends, or spending time outdoors.

In short, maintaining a clear mind requires a proactive approach. Through meditation, decluttering our environment, time management, exercise, healthy eating, adequate rest, the practice of letting go of control, gratitude, and limiting distractions, we can develop a clearer, calmer state of mind. These strategies help us not only think more clearly, but also face life with greater serenity and balance.

Taking care of your Physical Health

Taking care of your physical health is essential to achieving a balanced life. Although we often prioritize our responsibilities, work or family, it is important to remember that without good health, everything else becomes more difficult. Physical health is the foundation on which we can build our goals, relationships and daily activities. It is not just about avoiding illness, but about feeling strong, energetic and able to face whatever comes. When our body is in good shape, our mind also works better and we are able to make better decisions, think clearly and enjoy life more.

One of the fundamental pillars of taking care of your physical health is regular exercise. You don't have to become an athlete to stay fit, but it's crucial to move every day. The human body is designed to be in motion. When we spend a lot of time sitting or inactive, we start to feel sluggish, with little energy, and we can even develop long-term health problems. Exercising not only strengthens muscles and bones, but also improves the functioning of the heart, lungs, and circulatory system. In addition, when we exercise, our brain releases endorphins, which are chemicals that make us feel happier and less stressed. Walking, swimming, cycling, or even dancing are fun and effective ways to incorporate physical activity into our daily routine. The important thing is to find something you enjoy, so that you stay consistent and don't see it as an obligation, but as time to take care of yourself.

Another important part of physical care is nutrition. What we eat has a direct impact on our energy, how we feel, and our long-term health. A balanced diet doesn't mean depriving ourselves of the foods we love, but rather learning to choose options that nourish us and keep us strong. Eating a variety of fruits, vegetables, lean proteins, and whole grains can provide us with the nutrients our body needs to function at its best. On the other hand, ultra-processed foods, full of sugars and saturated fats, can make us feel heavy and tired, affecting not only our physical health, but also our mood. By paying attention to what we eat, we are feeding our body what it needs to perform at its best, allowing us to have enough energy to face the day with spirit and clarity.

Adequate rest is also a vital component of physical care. We often underestimate the importance of getting enough sleep, but sleep is essential for the body to recover and repair itself. When we sleep, our body works to heal tissues, strengthen the immune system, and recharge energy. If we don't get enough sleep, we feel tired, irritable, and our ability to concentrate and make decisions is impaired. Additionally, prolonged sleep deprivation can have serious health consequences, including an increased risk of heart disease, diabetes, and other chronic problems. Creating a sleep routine that allows us to get enough rest each night is key to maintaining good physical health. This includes avoiding screens before bed, maintaining a regular sleep schedule, and making sure our bedroom is a comfortable, calm space where we can relax.

Hydration is another aspect that we cannot overlook. Our body is composed mainly of water, and every cell, organ and system needs this vital liquid to function properly. Drinking enough water throughout the day helps us maintain our energy levels, keep our muscles and joints working smoothly and our skin healthy. Often, fatigue or headaches can be signs that we are not well hydrated. The key is to make hydration a daily habit. Although the amount of water we need varies from person to person, a good starting point is to make sure we drink water regularly and not wait until we are thirsty to do so.

Stress management is also essential to taking care of your physical health. Chronic stress can take a serious toll on your body, causing problems like headaches, muscle tension, digestive issues, and heart disease. While we can't always avoid stressful situations, we can learn to manage them in healthier ways. Exercise, meditation, deep breathing, and relaxing activities like reading or spending time with loved ones are all great ways to reduce stress levels. Taking care of our mental and emotional health is just as important as taking care of our bodies, as the two are deeply connected.

Another aspect of physical care that is often overlooked is the importance of regular medical checkups. As we age, it is critical to stay on top of our health and catch potential problems before they become more serious. This includes going to the doctor for general checkups, getting blood tests, checking blood pressure, and making sure everything is working properly. Prevention is the best medicine, and by staying vigilant about our health we can avoid complications down the road. Sometimes small changes in our lifestyle, such as adjusting our diet or incorporating more physical activity, can make a big difference in our overall health.

Taking care of our body also means being aware of the signals it sends us. Often, the body tells us when something is not right, whether through pain, fatigue or discomfort. Listening to our body is a way to prevent bigger problems. If we feel persistent pain, lack of energy or any other unusual symptoms, it is important not to ignore it and seek the necessary help. The body is wise and gives us clues about what it needs to stay balanced, but it is up to us to pay attention and act accordingly.

It is also essential to find a balance between work and rest. Many people believe that in order to be successful they must work non-stop, sacrificing their physical well-being. However, rest is part of the productivity process. If we do not give the body the time it needs to recover, we will eventually become exhausted and our health will suffer. Taking breaks, disconnecting from work and allowing ourselves moments of relaxation is not a luxury, but a necessity. A tired body cannot perform at its best, and if we want to achieve our goals, we must ensure that we are taking care of our physical health along the way.

Finally, taking care of your physical health doesn't have to be overwhelming or complicated. Small changes in our daily habits can have a big impact on our long-term health. It's not about following a strict diet or doing extreme exercises, but about adopting healthy habits that we can maintain over time. The key is to be consistent and make physical care a natural part of our daily routine. This will allow us to enjoy a fuller life, with energy and well-being, and will help us face challenges with more strength and resilience.

In short, taking care of our physical health is an investment in our quality of life. Through regular exercise, a balanced diet, adequate rest, hydration, stress management, medical check-ups, and listening to our own body, we can stay strong and healthy. These habits not only improve our physical health, but also contribute to a clearer mind and emotional well-being. By taking care of our body, we are building a solid foundation for a balanced and fulfilling life.

Anna Baker

Finding the Middle Ground

Finding the middle ground in life may sound simple, but it's actually one of the hardest things to achieve. We live in a society where we're often pushed to extremes. We're told that we need to work longer hours to be successful, that we need to eat super healthy, or that we need to always be the best at everything we do. However, what really brings us well-being and balance is finding that middle ground, that place where we're neither too far to one side nor too far to the other, but right in the middle. That point of balance allows us to live in a more peaceful way and enjoy things without exhausting ourselves or feeling pressured all the time.

When we talk about finding the middle ground, it doesn't mean that everything in our lives should be measured with a perfect ruler or that we should live in a strict routine. It's more about knowing when it's time to push ourselves and when it's time to rest, when we should indulge ourselves and when we should be more conscious of our choices. This balance applies to all areas of our lives: from food, work, relationships, to the time we spend on ourselves. Finding the middle ground is an art that requires self-knowledge and constant practice, because it's not always easy to recognize when we're leaning too far to one side.

In the workplace, for example, it's easy to fall into the extreme of working non-stop or, on the contrary, not putting in enough effort. The middle ground here would be learning to manage our time so that we can meet our responsibilities without sacrificing our personal well-being. It's important to have goals and be productive, but it's also necessary to have time to rest, to enjoy life and recharge our energy. If we only focus on work and leave our personal life aside, sooner or later we'll feel exhausted and frustrated. But if we relax too much and don't give our obligations the necessary attention, we can also end up feeling dissatisfied and stagnant. The middle ground here would be finding a balance between being productive and giving ourselves permission to disconnect and enjoy other things that make us happy.

When it comes to food, finding the middle ground means allowing ourselves to enjoy the foods we love without going into overindulgence or extreme deprivation. If we stick to a very strict diet all the time, we'll probably end up feeling deprived and frustrated, which can lead to binge eating or abandoning our healthy habits altogether. On the other hand, if we don't pay attention to what we eat and just indulge in cravings and unnutritious foods, our health will suffer. The middle ground is learning to enjoy food in a balanced way, eating healthily most of the time, but also giving ourselves those little treats that make us happy. It's not about being perfect, but about finding a lifestyle that we can maintain in the long term, without feeling deprived or guilty.

In our personal relationships, finding the middle ground is also crucial. Sometimes, we can fall into the extreme of wanting to please others all the time, sacrificing our own needs and desires. Or, on the contrary, we can be too selfish, thinking only of ourselves without considering how our actions affect others. The middle ground in this case would be finding a balance between taking care of our own needs and being aware of the needs of others. It is important to set healthy boundaries and make sure that our relationships are balanced, where both we and others are respected and valued. By finding this balance, our relationships will be more harmonious and satisfying.

Time for ourselves is also an area where we need to find a middle ground. We live in a time when many people feel guilty about taking time for themselves, whether it is to rest, to do something they enjoy, or simply to relax. But it is essential to have moments of self-care, where we can disconnect from the outside world and recharge our energies. However, it is also important not to fall into the other extreme, where we isolate ourselves too much or neglect our responsibilities. The middle ground would be to find moments in our daily routine where we can take time for ourselves without feeling guilty, but also make sure to fulfill our obligations and stay connected with the people around us.

The balance between effort and rest is key in all areas of life. Sometimes, excessive effort leads to exhaustion and a feeling that we are constantly chasing something without ever enjoying the journey. On the other hand, excessive rest can make us feel apathetic or disconnected from our own goals. The middle ground would be learning to work hard when necessary, but also allowing ourselves to rest and recharge when our body or mind needs it. This balance is especially important to avoid physical and emotional exhaustion, which is crucial to maintaining a balanced and fulfilling life.

In the quest for balance, it's also important to recognize that life won't always be perfect, and there will be times when we lean more toward one side than the other. That's okay. It's not always possible to be exactly in the middle all the time, and the most important thing is to be flexible and aware of when adjustments need to be made. Sometimes life requires us to put more effort into certain areas, such as when we're working on an important project or going through a difficult situation. At those times, it's normal for some other areas of our life to take a backseat. The important thing is to recognize when it's time to rebalance the scales and make sure that, in the long run, we're finding a rhythm that allows us to maintain that balance.

Finding the middle ground also involves being compassionate with ourselves. We're not always going to have everything under control, and it's okay to make mistakes or go off track from time to time. The important thing is to learn from those experiences and continue to seek balance. Life is a continuous process of adjustment and adaptation, and each of us has our own pace and our own challenges. By being kind to ourselves and accepting that balance is not something static, but something we're constantly cultivating, we can live more relaxed and fulfilling lives.

In short, finding the middle ground in life is a skill that requires practice and awareness. It's about avoiding extremes and seeking a balance that allows us to live more peacefully and fully. Whether it's at work, in our diet, in our relationships, or in our time for ourselves, balance helps us feel more satisfied and avoid burnout or frustration. It's not about being perfect, but about finding a lifestyle that allows us to enjoy the things we care about without feeling overwhelmed or deprived. The middle ground is the place where we can live with more peace, harmony, and well-being.

Creating Balanced Connections

Creating balanced connections is one of the most important aspects of maintaining a harmonious and fulfilling life. The relationships we form with the people around us, whether they are family, friends, coworkers, or partners, play a fundamental role in our emotional and mental well-being. However, achieving healthy and balanced connections can be a challenge. Many times, we fall into extremes: we give too much of ourselves, we worry more about pleasing others, or, on the contrary, we disconnect emotionally and do not put in the necessary effort to nurture those relationships. Finding balance in our connections means learning to give and receive, to set healthy boundaries, and to be aware of our own needs without neglecting those of others.

A balanced connection is one in which both parties feel heard, respected, and valued. This doesn't mean that every interaction has to be perfect or that there won't be disagreements, but that both people feel on equal footing to express what they think and feel. In an unbalanced relationship, one person may feel like they're always giving more, that their needs aren't being met, or that they don't have the space to truly be who they are. These types of relationships can lead to emotional exhaustion and frustration. On the other hand, if we only focus on receiving without giving, the other person may end up feeling used or undervalued. Therefore, the key is to find a middle ground where both parties contribute to the growth and well-being of the relationship.

One of the most important aspects of creating balanced connections is communication. The way we talk to others and how we listen to what they have to say is critical to building a healthy relationship. Sometimes, lack of communication or poor communication can cause misunderstandings and resentments. That's why it's crucial to learn to express ourselves clearly and honestly, but also in a respectful way. Being honest doesn't mean being hurtful or insensitive, but rather saying what we think and feel in a way that invites dialogue, not confrontation. In the same way, active listening is essential. It's not just about hearing what the other person is saying, but really paying attention and trying to understand their point of view, even if we don't agree. When both people in a relationship feel heard and valued, it's much easier to maintain a healthy balance.

Another important part of balanced connections is respect for personal boundaries. We all need space and time for ourselves, and it's critical that the people in our lives understand and respect those boundaries. This can be difficult in some relationships, especially when we're very close to someone or when the other person is very dependent on us. However, setting clear boundaries is not only beneficial for our own mental health, but also for the relationship itself. When we set boundaries in a loving and respectful way, we're saying that we value the relationship enough to take care of it and make sure it doesn't become a source of stress or resentment. Setting boundaries doesn't mean distancing ourselves emotionally, but rather finding a balance where we can be present in the other person's life without feeling overwhelmed or sacrificing our own peace of mind.

Balance in relationships also involves being aware of our own needs and desires. We often get carried away by the need to please others, avoid conflict, or meet the expectations of those around us, and in the process we forget what we really need. This can lead us to resent the people we are connected to, even if we are not aware of it at first. To avoid this, it is essential to make an effort to reflect on what we really want and need in our relationships. Once we know this, it is important to communicate it openly and honestly. We should not be afraid to express our needs for fear that others will get upset or reject us. On the contrary, being clear about what we need helps us build more authentic and meaningful relationships.

However, balance doesn't just involve thinking about ourselves, but also about the needs of the other person. Sometimes, we can be so focused on our own concerns that we forget that the other person has their own desires, fears, and expectations, too. It's important to make a conscious effort to empathize with others, to try to understand what they're going through and how our actions can affect them. This kind of empathy not only strengthens relationships, but it also helps us find solutions that benefit both parties. In a balanced connection, both people are willing to compromise, give in when necessary, and find common ground.

The time we spend in our relationships also plays a key role in maintaining balance. Sometimes, we can be so busy with our daily responsibilities that we don't make time for the important people in our lives. Other times, we can focus so much on our relationships that we neglect other important areas, such as our work or self-care. Balance in connections means finding a middle ground, where we can be present for the people we care about without neglecting our own priorities. This can involve making a conscious effort to schedule quality time with the people we love, but also learning to say "no" when we need space for ourselves or when our responsibilities require it.

Another important aspect of creating balanced connections is being flexible and adapting to changes. Relationships are not static, they change over time as people grow and evolve. What worked in a relationship at one point in time may not work in the future. Being aware of this allows us to be more flexible and adapt to changes without feeling threatened or insecure. Part of balance in relationships is understanding that we can't always control what happens, but we can control how we react and how we adapt to new circumstances. By being flexible, we can keep our relationships strong and healthy over time, even when things change.

Also, it's important to remember that not every relationship will be balanced all the time. There will be times when one person needs more support or more attention, and that's okay. Balance doesn't mean that everything is equal all the time, but rather that, overall, both people feel valued and respected. It's normal for a relationship to sometimes be more temporarily out of balance, either because one person is going through a difficult time or because circumstances have changed. The important thing is that both people are willing to work together to restore balance when necessary.

In short, creating balanced connections is an ongoing process that requires effort and attention. It involves communicating clearly and respectfully, setting healthy boundaries, being aware of our own needs, and empathizing with the needs of others. It also means being flexible and adaptable to change, dedicating quality time to our relationships without neglecting other important areas of our lives. By finding this balance, we can build more meaningful and fulfilling relationships, which bring us well-being and happiness over time. Balanced connections not only enrich our lives, but also help us grow and evolve as people, creating a virtuous cycle of mutual support and emotional well-being.

The Key to Reconnecting with Yourself

Finding yourself is one of the most important and challenging tasks in life. In the hustle and bustle of daily life, we often get caught up in the expectations of others, the responsibilities life imposes on us, or even the versions of ourselves we think we should be. All of this can make us feel disconnected from who we really are, from our passions, our desires, and our deepest values. The key to finding yourself is to take the time and effort to get to know yourself, understand your true needs, and live in accordance with them. This is not a quick or easy process, but it is essential to living an authentic and fulfilling life.

To start, it's crucial to take time for self-reflection. Often times, we're so busy with daily tasks and external demands that we don't give ourselves the space to think about what we really want and need. Taking time for self-reflection allows you to explore your deepest thoughts and feelings, which helps you better understand who you are. You can do this through meditation, journaling, or simply spending time in solitude. The idea is to create a space where you can be honest with yourself, without distractions or external pressures. By doing so, you begin to discover what truly makes you happy, what annoys you, and what you're passionate about, which is crucial to reconnecting with yourself.

Another important aspect is learning to listen to your intuition. Often, we ignore that little voice inside that guides us toward what we really want, because we are more focused on what is expected of us or what is practical. However, your intuition is a fundamental part of yourself, that knows your deepest desires and needs. Listening to and trusting your intuition can help you make decisions that are aligned with your true self. This may mean following a different path in your career, embracing new passions, or simply making changes in your daily life that bring you closer to who you really are. The key is to be brave and follow that inner guidance, even if it may sometimes feel risky or unconventional.

Reconnecting with yourself also involves letting go of expectations and judgments that you have placed on yourself or that others have placed on you. Often, we get caught up in the idea of how we should be instead of accepting and loving the person we really are. This can be especially difficult if you have been following a path that does not align with your true desires. However, freeing yourself from those expectations and judgments allows you to be more authentic. It is a process of acceptance and self-compassion, where you allow yourself to be yourself without having to conform to the standards that have been imposed on you. Accepting your imperfections and acknowledging your achievements is fundamental to reconnecting with your true self.

Self-knowledge is another key pillar to finding yourself again. Knowing yourself deeply helps you understand your strengths, weaknesses, values, and motivations. This involves exploring your interests and passions, as well as reflecting on your past experiences to learn from them. Sometimes, this may require stepping out of your comfort zone and trying new things. By facing different experiences and challenges, you may discover aspects of yourself that you were previously unaware of. This self-knowledge provides you with a solid foundation on which you can build a life that is aligned with who you really are.

It's also important to surround yourself with people who support and inspire you. The relationships you have can influence how you see yourself and how you feel about your life. Being around people who accept you and encourage you to be yourself can be a huge help in the process of finding yourself again. These people can offer you support, understanding, and perspectives that help you see your life from a different angle. Sometimes, the company of someone who truly understands you can be a great encouragement to you in recognizing and accepting yourself for who you are.

Additionally, it's crucial to set healthy boundaries. Often, in order to please others, we overload ourselves with commitments that don't reflect our true priorities or desires. Learning to say "no" and setting clear boundaries is a way to protect your time and energy so that you can devote yourself to what really matters to you. Not only does this help you maintain a healthy balance in your life, but it also allows you to focus on what truly makes you happy and brings you closer to your true self. Setting healthy boundaries also allows you to be more honest with yourself and others about your needs and expectations.

Self-care is another key aspect of finding yourself again. Taking time to look after your physical, emotional and mental wellbeing is essential to maintaining a healthy balance. This can include activities that relax you, motivate you and make you feel good about yourself. Self-care is not a luxury, but a necessity to maintain a genuine connection with yourself. Make sure you do things that you enjoy and that make you feel good, whether it's through exercise, art, reading or any other activity that you are passionate about.

Finally, remember that finding yourself again is an ongoing journey. It is not something that is achieved overnight, but rather a process that develops over time. There will be times when you feel more connected to yourself and other times when you feel like you have lost your way. The important thing is to keep moving forward with patience and perseverance. Every step you take towards a greater understanding of yourself is valuable and brings you closer to a life that is aligned with who you really are.

In short, the key to reconnecting with yourself lies in taking time for self-reflection, listening to your intuition, letting go of expectations and judgments, getting to know yourself deeply, surrounding yourself with supportive people, setting healthy boundaries, and practicing self-care. This process will allow you to live more authentically and fulfillingly, aligning your actions and decisions with your true desires and values. Although the journey can be challenging, each step toward a greater connection with yourself offers you the opportunity to live a fuller and more enriching life.

Anna Baker

Technology and Balance

Technology has transformed our lives in unimaginable ways. Today, technology is present in almost everything we do, from the way we work to how we communicate and entertain ourselves. We live in an age where smartphones, social media, email, and a myriad of apps keep us connected 24 hours a day. While technology has brought enormous benefits, it has also posed a great challenge: how can we maintain balance in a world where technology seems to absorb every minute of our time? This is an especially important topic for those seeking a balanced life, as excessive use of technology can throw off several aspects of our lives, such as our relationships, mental health, and overall well-being.

One of the first steps to achieving a healthy balance with technology is being aware of how and how much we use it. Often, we don't realize how much time we spend in front of a screen, whether it's our phone, computer, or TV. It's easy to get lost in social media, watch videos endlessly, or answer emails endlessly. This may seem harmless, but in the long run it can affect our productivity, our personal relationships, and our mental health. So it's important to stop and ask ourselves: am I using technology consciously or am I just getting carried away by it? The simple act of becoming aware of how much time we spend online can be the first step toward balance.

Another important aspect is setting boundaries with technology. Just like with anything else in life, too much can be harmful, and technology is no exception. One of the biggest challenges we face today is that technology is designed to be addictive. Constant notifications, social media that never stops, and the need to always be available can make us feel like we never have a moment to rest. To find a balance, setting clear boundaries is essential. For example, we can set specific times to check our social media or emails, or decide not to use our phone during meals or right before bed. These boundaries allow us to regain control over our time and prevent technology from invading every aspect of our life.

Digital rest is another key concept to maintaining a balance with technology. Just as our body needs rest after a day of physical activity, our mind also needs to disconnect from screens. Spending too much time in front of devices can lead to mental fatigue, concentration problems, and even insomnia. A good strategy is to schedule regular breaks throughout the day to get away from screens. This can be as simple as getting up every hour for a few minutes, going for a walk, stretching, or simply closing your eyes and taking a deep breath. These breaks not only help us reduce fatigue, but they also improve our productivity and overall well-being.

Technology can also affect our personal relationships if we don't manage it properly. It's common to see people sitting at the same table, each looking at their phone instead of talking to each other. While technology connects us with people who are far away, it can also disconnect us from those who are close by. To maintain a balance, it's important to be aware of how technology impacts our daily interactions. We can, for example, decide not to use our phones when we're in the company of friends or family, or at least reduce our use of them so that our interactions are more meaningful. By putting our attention on the people we're with and not on our screens, we can strengthen our relationships and live more authentic moments.

Another important aspect of technology and balance is how it affects our physical health. Spending long hours in front of a computer or phone can have negative consequences for our body. Incorrect posture, lack of movement, and constant eye strain are just some of the problems that can arise. To counteract these effects, it is essential to incorporate movement into our daily lives. This can include small stretching exercises, getting up from time to time to walk around, or adjusting our posture to avoid back pain. In addition, it is important to take care of our eyes by taking regular breaks from screens and adjusting the brightness and lighting to reduce eye fatigue.

Balancing technology also means being selective about the information we consume. In the digital age, we are constantly bombarded with news, opinions, videos, and an endless amount of content that can be overwhelming. This excess of information, often referred to as "information overload," can lead to anxiety, confusion, and stress. To avoid this, it is important to be more aware of what type of information we choose to consume. We can select reliable sources, limit the time we spend on social media, or decide not to watch news that only causes us distress. By being more selective about what we watch and read, we can protect our mental health and maintain a more positive attitude.

One of the great things about technology is that it can also be a powerful tool for well-being if we use it correctly. There are many apps designed to help us meditate, exercise, improve our diet, or even organize our time more efficiently. Instead of seeing technology as an enemy, we can learn to use it intelligently to our advantage. For example, if we struggle to find time to exercise, we can use an app to help us establish daily routines. Or if we have difficulty relaxing, we can take advantage of the many meditation or relaxing sound apps out there. The key is to use technology as a tool to help us improve our lives, and not as something that controls us.

Technology can also be an ally in keeping us connected in a positive way. While it can certainly throw our relationships out of balance if we don't manage it well, it also allows us to stay in touch with people we might not otherwise see. In times when it's not possible to be physically close to our loved ones, technology gives us the opportunity to maintain those connections. The important thing is to use it consciously, making sure that the interactions we have online are meaningful and not just another distraction. Calling a friend to check in, sending a message of support, or having a video call with family are all ways in which technology can enrich our relationships rather than harm them.

Finally, it is important to recognize that balance with technology is not about eliminating it from our lives. Technology is an integral part of our modern world, and it offers countless benefits. What we need to strive for is to find a middle ground where we can enjoy the advantages it offers us without sacrificing our well-being. This involves setting boundaries, being mindful of our use, unplugging when necessary, and using technology in positive and constructive ways. By doing so, we can integrate technology into our lives in a way that helps us live more balanced and fulfilling lives.

In short, technology plays an important role in our lives, but it is crucial to find a balance so that it does not become a source of stress or disconnection. Setting boundaries, taking digital breaks, taking care of our physical and mental health, and using technology consciously and selectively are key steps to achieving this balance. In the end, technology can be a powerful tool for our well-being if we learn to manage it in a smart and balanced way.

Anna Baker

The Art of Saying No

Saying "no" is an art that many people find difficult to master. We live in a society that often values accommodating and always being there for others. From a young age, we are taught to be kind, to help others, and to not disappoint the expectations others have of us. While these are positive qualities, they can also become a problem when they lead us to say "yes" to things we don't really want to do, simply out of fear of rejection or not wanting to displease. Learning to say "no" is an essential skill for maintaining a balanced life and protecting our well-being. It's not about being selfish or pushing others away, but about recognizing our own needs and limits.

One of the most common reasons we have a hard time saying "no" is because we want to avoid conflict. We fear that by refusing to do something, the other person will feel offended, disappointed, or upset. What we often don't realize, however, is that by saying "yes" to everything, we often put ourselves in situations where we feel exhausted, stressed, or even resentful. Saying "no" clearly and respectfully is a way to take care of ourselves. It allows us to prioritize our own needs and ensure that we're not compromising our mental or physical peace just to please others. By doing so, we're not only protecting ourselves, but we're also being more authentic in our relationships since we're not saying "yes" just out of commitment or obligation.

The first step in learning to say "no" is to recognize that we can't always do everything. Our energy and time are limited, and if we try to take on too much, we end up burning ourselves out. It's important to be realistic about our capabilities and recognize when something is overwhelming us. This means being honest with ourselves and accepting that it's okay not to be able to do everything. We're not superheroes, and it's okay to prioritize what's really important to us. When we understand this, we realize that saying "no" isn't a failure, but rather a way of taking care of ourselves.

Another fundamental aspect of the art of saying "no" is learning to do so without feeling guilty. Guilt is one of the emotions that paralyzes us the most when we try to set boundaries. We feel like we are being selfish or that we are letting others down if we do not agree to their requests. However, it is essential to remember that saying "no" does not mean that you do not care about other people. On the contrary, many times, by setting boundaries, we are avoiding situations that in the long term could generate more resentment or frustration. Saying "no" from a position of respect and clarity is a healthy way to protect your space and your well-being without damaging relationships.

One of the best ways to say "no" without feeling bad is to learn to do it in a polite but firm way. There's no need to give long explanations or justifications about why you can't do something. A simple "no, thank you" or "no, I can't right now" is enough. Many times, we try to justify our refusal with too many details, which can open the door for others to try to convince us to change our mind. Keeping the answer simple and clear is an effective way to set your boundaries without getting into unnecessary arguments. Also, remember that you're not obligated to give reasons every time you refuse to do something. Your time and energy are yours, and you have the right to decide how you use them.

The art of saying "no" also involves practicing it regularly. At first, it may feel awkward or even scary, but like any other skill, you will improve with practice. Start with small situations where you feel comfortable saying "no" and gradually apply it to other aspects of your life. Over time, you will notice that it not only becomes easier, but you will also begin to feel a greater sense of control over your life and well-being. Saying "no" will help you feel freer and less burdened by commitments that do not bring you anything positive.

It's also important to recognize that saying "no" is a form of respect for others. Although it may seem counterintuitive, setting clear boundaries prevents misunderstandings and resentments down the road. When we agree to do things we don't want to do, we're more likely to do them reluctantly or without the necessary enthusiasm. This can affect the quality of what we do or even our relationships. On the other hand, when we say "no" from the beginning, we're being honest and transparent, which in the long run strengthens trust in our relationships.

Another benefit of learning to say "no" is that it allows you to focus on what really matters. When you say "yes" to everything, you end up spending your time on tasks that aren't always important to you. This can leave you feeling drained and like you're not making progress toward your own goals. By saying "no" to certain things, you're creating space in your life for what you're truly passionate about, what makes you feel fulfilled, and what allows you to grow. Not only is this approach beneficial for your personal well-being, it also improves your productivity and helps you achieve your goals more effectively.

Saying "no" also has a positive impact on your mental health. When you overload yourself with responsibilities, your mind suffers as you are constantly thinking about everything you have to do and how to meet the expectations of others. This pressure can lead to anxiety, stress, and even sleep problems. By learning to say "no," you reduce this mental burden and allow yourself to relax and focus on what really matters to you. Simply knowing that you don't have to do everything for everyone frees you from a lot of stress.

Finally, it's important to remember that saying "no" is an act of self-love. It's a way of honoring your boundaries, your needs, and your desires. It's not about being selfish or pushing others aside, but rather making sure that you're not neglecting yourself in the process of helping others. When you take care of yourself and prioritize yourself, you're also in a better position to help others genuinely and from a place of well-being. Balance in life isn't about doing it all, but rather knowing when and how to say "no" to protect what's truly important to you.

In short, the art of saying "no" is an essential skill for maintaining a balanced and healthy life. It involves recognizing your limits, being honest with yourself and others, and learning to put your own needs first. It is not an act of selfishness, but of self-care and respect for yourself and those around you. Practicing saying "no" will help you free up time and energy for the things that really matter, reducing stress and improving your overall well-being. In the end, learning to say "no" clearly and respectfully is one of the most powerful tools for living a fuller and more balanced life.

Anna Baker

Finances in Balance

Having a balanced finance is one of the most important pillars to achieving a balanced life. Financial stress can often affect other aspects of our lives, such as mental health, personal relationships, and even our physical well-being. Constant worries about money can lead to anxiety, worry, and a feeling of lack of control over our future. Therefore, learning to manage our finances in a balanced way is key to maintaining a calm and stable life. This chapter explores the importance of balanced finances and how we can achieve them, even when it seems complicated.

The first step to having balanced finances is to understand our current financial situation. Many people avoid looking at their bank accounts or debts for fear of what they will find. However, to improve our finances, we need to be honest with ourselves and clearly assess where they are. This means reviewing how much money we earn, how much we spend, and how much we owe. While it may be uncomfortable to face reality, it is the only way to start working on improving our finances. By knowing exactly where we stand, we can make more informed decisions and avoid unpleasant surprises in the future.

Once we understand our financial situation, the next step is to learn how to budget. A budget is a simple yet powerful tool that allows us to have control over our income and expenses. Often, when we don't have a clear plan for our money, it's easy to overspend or lose track of where our paycheck is going. By creating a budget, we're telling our money where to go instead of just mindlessly spending it. To make a budget, we can start by dividing our expenses into categories like food, housing, transportation, entertainment, and savings. This way, we can clearly see which areas we're spending more on and which areas we could cut back on. A budget not only helps us control our spending, but it also allows us to plan for the future.

Saving is another essential component of balanced finances. We often think of saving as something we can only do if we have a high salary or if we have money left over at the end of the month. However, saving is not about how much money we earn, but about the discipline we have to set aside a portion of our income, no matter how small. Saving allows us to be prepared for unexpected events, such as a medical emergency or a home repair, and it also gives us the ability to meet long-term goals, such as a trip, buying a house, or educating our children. To start saving, we can set realistic and achievable goals. It doesn't matter if we start by saving a small amount each month, the important thing is to create the habit. Over time, those savings will grow and give us a greater sense of financial security.

A key concept to keep your finances in balance is learning to differentiate between needs and wants. Many times, we spend money on things we don't really need, just because they seem attractive at the time or because we feel external pressure, whether social or advertising, to have them. This is one of the main reasons why people get into debt or feel like they don't have enough money, since they spend a significant part of their income on things that are not essential. To achieve a better balance, it is important to pause before making any purchase and ask ourselves if we really need what we want to buy or if it is just a passing desire. This simple reflection can help us avoid unnecessary purchases and keep our finances under control.

Debt management is also crucial for balanced finances. Living with debt can be one of the main sources of financial stress, especially if the debts grow and seem to never end. While in some cases debt is unavoidable, such as when buying a house or a vehicle, it is important to learn to manage it responsibly. The key is not to go into debt beyond what we can pay. If we already have debts, it is essential to prioritize their payment before taking on new financial commitments. We can start by paying off debts with higher interest or those that generate a larger monthly burden. In addition, it is advisable to avoid excessive use of credit cards, since high interest can cause our debts to grow quickly. Controlling debts not only gives us peace of mind, but also allows us to have greater financial freedom.

Another way to keep our finances balanced is by diversifying our sources of income. Many people rely solely on a fixed salary, which can be risky if something changes, such as losing a job or reducing work hours. Diversifying our income means finding additional ways to make money, whether through our own business, investments, or a project we can do in our free time. Not only does this give us greater financial stability, but it also allows us to be better prepared for any unforeseen events.

Financial education is essential to achieving balance in our finances. Many times, we make financial decisions without really understanding how economic systems work or how they affect our long-term choices. That's why it's important to spend time learning about personal finance, saving, investing, and debt management. Today, there are many resources available, from books and articles to videos and online courses, that can help us improve our financial knowledge. Financial education gives us the tools we need to make smarter decisions and avoid mistakes that could undermine our stability.

Finally, it is important to remember that financial balance is not just about accumulating money, but knowing how to use it in a way that brings us well-being and peace of mind. Money is a tool that allows us to live more comfortably, but it should not become a source of anguish or constant worry. By learning to manage our finances in a balanced way, we can enjoy our present more and have greater security for the future. This does not mean that we do not have to make sacrifices or adjustments, but by doing so, we will be building a solid foundation for a more balanced and peaceful life.

In short, maintaining a balanced finances involves understanding our financial situation, creating and following a budget, saving in a disciplined manner, managing our debts responsibly, diversifying our income, and educating ourselves about personal finances. With these steps, we can reduce financial stress, be better prepared for unforeseen events, and enjoy a more fulfilling life. Financial balance is not something that is achieved overnight, but with perseverance and patience, it is possible to achieve it and maintain it over the long term.

The Power of Gratitude

Gratitude is one of the most powerful tools we have to maintain balance in our lives, yet we often overlook it. Sometimes we are so focused on the things we lack or what is not going well that we forget to stop and appreciate all that we already have. Gratitude is not just about being polite and saying thank you, but about having a conscious attitude of recognition towards the good things, big or small, that are present in our lives. Practicing gratitude helps us see the world from a more positive perspective, which has a direct impact on our happiness and well-being.

One of the most notable effects of gratitude is that it helps us focus on what we have, rather than what we lack. Often, we are so caught up in the race to get more things, more success, or more recognition, that we don't realize that we already have many reasons to feel lucky. When we practice gratitude, we shift our focus and begin to value what is already present in our lives. This doesn't mean that we should settle for what we have and stop aspiring to grow, but it allows us to do so from a place of peace and satisfaction, rather than frustration or emptiness.

Gratitude also has a very positive impact on our emotions. When we take the time to reflect on the things we are grateful for, our minds become filled with positive and constructive thoughts. This, in turn, helps us reduce stress, anxiety, and feelings of being overwhelmed. Instead of focusing on problems or difficulties, gratitude invites us to recognize the blessings that already exist, which creates a sense of calm and well-being. It is almost as if gratitude is a natural antidote to stress, helping us see life with greater clarity and optimism.

Another benefit of gratitude is that it connects us more deeply with others. When we express gratitude towards the people in our lives, we are strengthening our relationships. We all want to feel valued and appreciated, and when we thank others for their support, their company, or their acts of kindness, we are creating a stronger bond. Furthermore, gratitude fosters an environment of generosity and reciprocity. When we thank someone, we are not only acknowledging what they have done for us, but we are also motivating them to continue being kind and to continue that positive energy. Gratitude, therefore, has a multiplier effect on our relationships, making them healthier and more fulfilling.

Practicing gratitude doesn't take a lot of effort or time. One of the simplest ways to cultivate it is to take a few minutes each day to reflect on the things we're grateful for. It can be something as simple as having a good day, enjoying a delicious meal, or receiving a call from a friend. We can also feel gratitude for deeper things, like having a roof over our heads, enjoying good health, or having supportive loved ones. The important thing is to make gratitude a daily habit. By taking a few minutes each day to focus on the positive, we begin to reprogram our minds to be more attentive to the good things around us.

Another interesting aspect of the power of gratitude is that it not only improves our emotional health, but also our physical health. Numerous studies have shown that people who practice gratitude regularly experience fewer symptoms of illness, sleep better, and have a better overall quality of life. This is because gratitude reduces stress and anxiety, which has a direct effect on our body. When we are less stressed, our immune system works better, which helps us stay healthier. Plus, gratitude motivates us to take better care of ourselves, as we appreciate our physical well-being more.

In difficult times, it can feel complicated to practice gratitude. When we are going through stress, loss, or disappointment, focusing on the positive can feel nearly impossible. However, it is precisely in those moments that gratitude becomes most powerful. Instead of getting stuck in negativity, gratitude allows us to find some light amidst the darkness. We may not be able to change the situation itself, but there is always something we can be grateful for, even in the toughest times. Maybe it is the support of a friend, the lesson learned through difficulty, or the simple ability to keep going. Practicing gratitude in times of adversity gives us the strength to keep going and helps us find hope when it seems like all is lost.

An effective way to incorporate gratitude into our lives is to keep a gratitude journal. This can be a notebook in which, every night, we write down three things we are grateful for that day. It doesn't matter how small or big those things are, the important thing is to take the time to acknowledge them. Over time, this exercise becomes a powerful tool to change our mindset and keep us focused on the positive. Even on days when everything seems to be going wrong, finding three things to be grateful for helps us put things into perspective and remember that there is always something good in our lives.

Gratitude also helps us live more fully in the present. Often, we get stuck in the past, worrying about mistakes or regrets, or in the future, anticipating problems or situations that haven't happened yet. Gratitude anchors us in the here and now, reminding us that the present is all we really have. By appreciating what's happening right now, whether it's a conversation with a loved one, a walk in nature, or a quiet moment, we're living more consciously. This helps us enjoy life more and reduce anxiety about what's out of our control.

It's important to remember that gratitude isn't something that just happens automatically; it's an intentional practice. It requires us to make a conscious effort to stop and reflect on what we have, rather than what we lack. At first, it may feel strange or forced, especially if we're not used to doing it. But over time, it becomes second nature, a way of looking at life from a more positive and grateful perspective.

In short, gratitude is a powerful tool that can transform our lives. It helps us focus on the positive, improve our relationships, reduce stress, and live more fully. It doesn't require great efforts, just a change in our mindset and the willingness to recognize the blessings, big or small, that we already have. By practicing gratitude, we not only improve our emotional and physical well-being, but we also create an environment of positivity and generosity around us. Ultimately, gratitude has the power to balance our lives and make us happier.

Anna Baker

The Path to Balance

The path to balance is certainly a journey that we all must undertake at some point in our lives. It is not an easy or straight path, let alone one with a clear end, but it is a constant process of adjustments, learning and improvement. Balance is not something that is achieved overnight; it is a daily practice, a continuous act of finding harmony between our responsibilities, our personal needs and our aspirations. Often, imbalance in our lives occurs because we are too focused on one particular area, such as work, relationships or social life, while other areas are neglected. Therefore, the real challenge is to learn to manage all these parts so that none of them overwhelms the others.

The first step on this path is self-awareness. We cannot achieve balance if we are not aware of what is throwing us off balance. Often, we live on autopilot, reacting to the demands of everyday life without stopping to evaluate what we really need. To find balance, it is crucial to stop and reflect on what aspects of our life are out of balance. Are we spending too much time on work and not enough on our personal relationships? Are we neglecting our physical or mental health? Self-awareness allows us to identify these points of imbalance so that we can begin to work on them consciously.

Once we have identified the areas that need attention, the next step is to prioritize. We can't do everything at once, nor should we try to. Balance doesn't mean that each area of our life gets exactly the same amount of attention at all times, but rather that we are prioritizing what really matters. This can vary at different stages of life. For example, at some times, work may need more attention, while at other times, our health or relationships need to be front and center. Learning to prioritize is essential to maintaining balance over the long term, as it allows us to adjust our energies and efforts in ways that don't leave us feeling drained or overwhelmed.

One of the keys on the path to balance is learning to say "no" when necessary. Often, we feel pressured to meet the expectations of others or to accept responsibilities that are not ours. However, saying "yes" to everything can lead us to a state of exhaustion and overload. Learning to say "no" does not mean being selfish or irresponsible; it means setting healthy boundaries to protect our well-being and stay focused on what really matters. This can be difficult at first, especially if we are used to wanting to please others, but over time we will realize that setting boundaries gives us the energy and space necessary to focus on what truly nourishes and balances us.

Balance also involves taking care of ourselves, both physically and emotionally. Often, we sacrifice our personal well-being in the name of work, family, or daily responsibilities. However, we cannot maintain balance if we are constantly exhausted or neglected. Part of the path to balance is making sure we are taking care of our own needs. This can mean taking time to exercise, getting adequate rest, practicing meditation, or simply enjoying activities that make us feel good. Self-care is not a luxury; it is an essential part of being able to function in a balanced way in all areas of our lives.

Another important aspect of balance is accepting that change is inevitable. Our lives are constantly evolving, and what works for us at one point in time may not work at another. Balance is not a static thing; it is a dynamic process that requires ongoing adjustments. Sometimes, we need to be flexible and willing to change our routines or priorities to adapt to new circumstances. This may mean making adjustments to our work schedule, rearranging our responsibilities at home, or changing the way we think about certain aspects of life. The key is to be flexible and not hold on to a rigid idea of what balance should look like.

Balance is also about our relationships. Often, imbalance in our lives comes from relationships that are toxic or unbalanced. It's important to surround ourselves with people who support us and help us grow, rather than those who drain us or cause us stress. Learning to identify which relationships nourish us and which ones harm us is essential to maintaining emotional balance. Sometimes this means setting boundaries with certain people, or in some cases, walking away from relationships that are unhealthy. By nurturing our relationships in a balanced way, we are investing in our emotional and mental well-being.

On the path to balance, it's also important to recognize that we're not perfect and we won't always maintain balance all the time. There will be days when we feel out of balance, when work feels overwhelming or personal responsibilities overwhelm us. The important thing is not to beat ourselves up for those moments and instead see them as opportunities to readjust. Balance isn't about doing everything right all the time, but about finding a way to bounce back and return to a state of harmony when things get out of hand. Self-compassion is key in this process. Instead of being hard on ourselves for mistakes or imbalances, we can learn to be kind and understand that the path to balance is an ongoing journey, not a final destination.

It's also important not to compare our path to balance to that of others. Every person has their own pace, their own challenges, and their own priorities. What works for one person may not work for another, and that's okay. Balance is a personal thing, and each of us must find a way to achieve it in our own life, according to our circumstances and values. Comparing ourselves to others will only lead to frustration and push us away from our own balance. Instead of looking outward, it's important to focus on what we need to feel balanced and fulfilled in our own life.

Finally, the path to balance also involves learning to enjoy the present. Often, imbalance arises when we are too focused on the future or worried about what will come. Learning to be present, to enjoy the moments we have now, is essential to maintaining balance. This doesn't mean we shouldn't plan or aspire for more, but that we can't lose sight of what we already have right now. Practicing gratitude, as we mentioned before, is a great way to anchor ourselves in the present and find satisfaction in what we've already accomplished.

In short, the path to balance is an ongoing process that requires self-awareness, prioritization, healthy boundaries, self-care, flexibility, and good relationship management. It is not an easy road, but it is one worth taking. As we move forward on this journey, we will learn to adjust, bounce back from difficult times, and find peace amidst the chaos. Balance is not an end goal, but rather a way to live more fully, consciously, and in harmony with ourselves and the world around us.

Anna Baker

Disconnect to Connect

In the modern world, we are more connected than ever. Technology allows us to be in touch with people around the world instantly, access endless information with just a click, and have constant entertainment at our fingertips. However, this constant external connection has created a problem: we have lost the ability to connect with ourselves and with what really matters. We live in an era where disconnecting seems to be a luxury, when in fact it is an urgent necessity for our mental, emotional, and even physical health. Disconnecting does not mean isolating ourselves completely or stopping using technology, but rather finding the balance necessary to reconnect with what is essential in our lives: our inner peace, our relationships, and our connection to the real world.

Disconnecting is harder than it seems because we are used to immediacy. We check our phones as soon as we wake up, we respond to messages within seconds, and we keep an eye on social media all day long. This routine has accustomed us to a cycle of constant distraction, where we find it difficult to spend time in silence or simply be present without the need to do something. The problem is that when we are always connected, our minds become filled with noise. The noise of notifications, news, and other people's lives constantly displayed on social media. All of this distances us from our own selves, from our true needs, and from the people in front of us.

In order to reconnect with ourselves and others, we must first learn to tune out all that noise. It's not easy, because we often feel a kind of anxiety about disconnecting. We worry about what we might miss, about not being aware of what's going on, or about not responding to someone right away. However, by consciously disconnecting, we are making space for what really matters. It's like cleaning up a messy room: by taking out the unnecessary, we find space to breathe, to think clearly, and to be more aware of what's around us.

Unplugging doesn't mean turning off your phone forever or stopping using technology altogether. It means setting healthy boundaries so that it doesn't overwhelm you. For example, we can unplug during certain times of the day, such as when we wake up, during meals, or before we sleep. These times are valuable for reconnecting with ourselves, reflecting on our day, or simply enjoying the present moment without the interference of a screen. At first, it may feel uncomfortable or difficult because we're so used to being constantly busy, but over time, it becomes a practice that brings us peace and clarity.

One of the great benefits of unplugging is that it allows us to reconnect with the people around us. Real-life relationships can suffer when we are too focused on digital connections. Maybe we've been at a gathering with friends or family and noticed that everyone is looking at their phones instead of enjoying the conversation. This has become commonplace, but it's no less damaging. True connection happens when we are present, when we look people in the eye, when we listen attentively, and when we take the time to share without distraction. By unplugging, we can have deeper, more meaningful relationships, and that authentic connection is an immense source of balance and happiness.

Another important aspect of unplugging is that it gives us the opportunity to reconnect with nature. Spending time outdoors, without the interference of technology, is one of the most powerful ways to restore our inner balance. Nature has a calming and revitalizing effect on us, but to fully experience it, we need to be present. When we are in nature and put our devices aside, we can appreciate the small wonders around us: the sound of birds, the wind in the trees, the smell of fresh air. These moments remind us of the simplicity and beauty of life – something we often forget when we are caught up in digital chaos.

In addition to improving our relationships and connecting with nature, unplugging is also critical for our mental health. Constant exposure to technology, especially social media, can negatively impact our self-esteem and emotional well-being. We see the "perfect" lives of others, leading us to compare ourselves and often feel like we don't measure up. This type of constant comparison can lead to stress, anxiety, and feelings of inadequacy. By disconnecting from these influences, we reduce the pressure to compare ourselves and can focus more on what truly makes us happy. It's in these moments of disconnection that we can evaluate our goals, our desires, and our emotions more clearly and without the influence of what's happening in the digital world.

Rest is also a key component of balance, and technology often interferes with our ability to get proper rest. It's not uncommon for many people to check their phones right before bed, which can make the wind-down process difficult. The light from screens affects our sleep cycle, and the constant stream of information keeps our minds active when they should be calming down. By unplugging before bed, we're allowing our body and mind to enter a state of deep rest, which is essential for our physical and mental health. Getting a good night's sleep is critical to keeping us balanced, and one of the best ways to improve our sleep is to create a wind-down routine before bed.

Unplugging also helps us reconnect with our passions and creativity. Often, we are so distracted by what is happening in the virtual world that we don't leave room to explore our own ideas or interests. Maybe you have a hobby that you have put aside because you can't find the time, or maybe you have a passion that you haven't had the chance to develop. By unplugging, we are creating space for those things that truly nourish us. We can dedicate time to reading, writing, painting, cooking, or any activity that we are passionate about, and that allows us to express ourselves authentically. Unplugging not only gives us time, but also the mental clarity necessary to focus on what really matters to us.

Ultimately, disconnecting to connect is a practice that requires intention and effort, but it has great benefits. By disconnecting from external noise, we give ourselves the opportunity to reconnect with ourselves, with our relationships, with nature, and with our passions. It's not about giving up technology completely, but rather learning to use it in a balanced way, without it consuming us. By creating healthy boundaries and making time to disconnect, we can live in a more full, present, and balanced way.

In a world that pushes us to always be connected, disconnecting becomes an act of self-care, a way to regain our energy and clarity. It's a reminder that while technology has an important place in our lives, it can't replace inner peace, genuine relationships, and connection to the real world. So, every once in a while, turn off your phone, close your computer, and give yourself the gift of reconnecting with what really matters.

Anna Baker

Balance in Changes

Balancing change is one of the biggest challenges we face in life. Change can be exciting and necessary, but it can also be overwhelming and destabilizing. Throughout our lives, we go through different stages that force us to adapt, whether it's a change at work, a move, a new relationship, or in some cases, the loss of something important. These changes, while sometimes unavoidable, can throw our sense of balance off course. The key is not to avoid change, but to learn how to manage it in a way that allows us to stay centered and balanced as we navigate it.

One of the first things we need to understand is that change is a natural part of life. Nothing stays the same forever, and although we sometimes wish things would stay stable, change is what allows us to grow and evolve. Resisting change only creates more stress and anxiety. When we accept that changes are inevitable, we can begin to see them as opportunities rather than threats. This mindset allows us to approach changes with a more positive and open attitude, making the adaptation process easier.

Maintaining balance in the midst of change means being emotionally prepared for transitions. This doesn't mean we have to have everything under control all the time, but we do need to learn to be flexible and adaptable. When something changes in our life, whether big or small, our initial reaction may be uncertainty or fear, but it's important to remember that we are capable of adapting. Flexibility is a skill we can develop over time, and the more open we are to change, the easier it will be to maintain balance as we face new situations.

Part of maintaining balance during change is learning to manage our emotions. Change, especially unexpected ones, can trigger a variety of emotions such as fear, sadness, frustration, or even euphoria. It's natural to feel this way, but the important thing is to not let ourselves be overwhelmed by these emotions. Instead of bottling up what we feel, we should allow ourselves to experience it and then work to find a way to process it in a healthy way. Talking to friends, family, or even journaling can help us put our emotions into perspective and keep a clear mind during the process of change.

Another key aspect of balancing change is planning. While we can't foresee every change that will occur in our lives, there are many that we can anticipate and prepare for. For example, if you know you're moving to a new city or starting a new job, you can start planning for the logistical and emotional aspects of the change. Making lists, establishing a plan of action, and having a clear idea of what the change will entail will give you a greater sense of control. This doesn't mean that everything will go exactly as you plan, but having a guide will allow you to feel more prepared and less vulnerable to unforeseen events.

In some cases, changes can be so significant that they profoundly alter our daily routine. Right now, it's essential to find a new normal as quickly as possible. One of the most effective ways to do this is by establishing new routines that allow you to feel a sense of stability. Even if everything in your life seems to be changing, maintaining certain habits and routines can help you feel more grounded. For example, if you used to exercise every morning, try to maintain that habit even in the midst of change. These small actions will provide you with a sense of continuity and control amidst uncertainty.

In addition to maintaining your routines, it's also important to find moments of calm and reflection during changes. Instead of rushing into decisions or figuring everything out right away, take the time to stop and breathe. Sometimes the best way to stay balanced during a change is to take a step back and assess the situation from a calmer, more objective perspective. Practicing meditation, deep breathing, or simply taking a few minutes a day to be quiet can help you calm your mind and see things more clearly.

Change also offers us the opportunity to rediscover our priorities. Often, we get caught up in the pace of life without stopping to think about what's really important to us. Change, while sometimes uncomfortable, allows us to reevaluate what we're doing and where we're going. Maybe a change at work makes you realize that you need more time for yourself or that it's time to put more energy into your personal relationships. Instead of seeing change as a disruption, you can see it as an opportunity to adjust your life so that it's more aligned with your values and desires.

It's natural to seek support from others during changes, and this is a good thing. Sometimes when we're in the middle of a transition, it's hard to see things clearly, and having the support of friends, family, or colleagues can make a huge difference. Don't hesitate to ask for help when you need it, whether it's to get advice, vent, or simply share your thoughts. Surrounding yourself with supportive people will give you the emotional and mental strength you need to stay balanced during difficult times.

It's also important to remember that not all change is negative. While some transitions can be painful or challenging, many changes bring with them new opportunities and experiences that can enrich our lives. Maybe a change at work leads you to discover a new passion, or a move allows you to meet people and places that inspire you. When we learn to view change as opportunities rather than obstacles, we open ourselves up to a world of possibilities we may not have considered before.

Maintaining balance during changes doesn't mean that everything will be easy or that you won't feel doubt or fear. It's normal to feel out of place at first, but over time, you'll begin to adapt and find your way through this new stage. Remember that balance is not a fixed state, but something we must continually adjust as we move through life. By facing changes with an open mind, a flexible attitude, and the right support, you'll be able to find your balance even in the most challenging situations.

Finally, keep in mind that changes are opportunities for growth. Every time you face change, you have the chance to learn something new about yourself, improve your stress management skills, and develop greater resilience. These moments of transition can be difficult, but they are also the ones that teach us the most valuable lessons. Instead of fearing change, try to embrace it as a natural part of life and an opportunity to become a stronger, more balanced version of yourself.

In short, balance in change is achieved through flexibility, planning, support, and acceptance of the unexpected. We can't control every aspect of our lives, but we can control how we respond to them. By keeping an open mind and adopting strategies that encourage self-care and reflection, we can navigate change with grace and balance.

Anna Baker

The Balance Between Giving and Receiving

The balance between giving and receiving is essential for a full and harmonious life. In our society, giving is often valued much more than receiving. We are taught that being generous and helping others is a noble act, and of course, it is. However, it is also important to recognize that receiving is equally necessary. Maintaining a healthy balance between these two actions is crucial for our emotional, mental, and physical well-being. If we only give and never receive, we are left empty; if we only receive and never give, we are disconnected from others. The trick is to find that middle ground where both actions complement each other and allow us to live in harmony.

Giving is something that is often associated with love, support, and generosity. We feel good when we help someone else, whether with our time, our skills, or simply our presence. Giving can be a source of joy, because it connects us to others and allows us to contribute to the well-being of those around us. However, if we give without measure, without taking care of ourselves in the process, we can burn out. Being generous doesn't mean always putting the needs of others above our own. To give genuinely and sustainably, we need to make sure our own reserves are full.

On the other hand, receiving can sometimes be harder than it seems. Many people feel guilty or uncomfortable accepting help or support from others, as if they were being selfish or dependent. However, the act of receiving is as natural as giving, and it is necessary to maintain a healthy balance in our relationships and in our lives. Accepting what others offer us is not a sign of weakness, but a way of recognizing that we also have needs, that we are not self-sufficient in everything, and that sometimes, we also need support. Learning to receive with gratitude and without guilt allows us to strengthen our relationships and teaches us to appreciate the generosity of others.

The balance between giving and receiving is a continual dance. Throughout our lives, there will be times when we give more and other times when we receive more, and that's okay. It's not about keeping an exact tally of who's giving and who's receiving, but about recognizing that both are essential to well-being. When we give, we do so from a place of abundance, knowing that we're contributing something valuable to others. And when we receive, we do so from a place of humility, recognizing that we can't always do it all on our own. This exchange is what creates a healthy, balanced relationship, both with others and with ourselves.

Often, people who are used to giving a lot find it difficult to accept help or even small gestures of support. They may feel more comfortable in the role of caregiver or problem solver, and have a hard time admitting that they need to receive, too. But the reality is that we all need to receive from time to time. No one can give indefinitely without burning out. By learning to accept what others have to offer us, we are creating a healthy cycle of energy, where what we give eventually comes back to us in some way. This cycle is what keeps us nourished, balanced, and able to keep going.

A simple example of this balance can be seen in our everyday relationships. Imagine two friends who constantly support each other. One day, one of them needs comfort, and the next day, it is the other who needs help. Neither of them is always in the role of giving or always in the role of receiving. They support each other according to the needs of the moment, which strengthens their bond and allows them to maintain a healthy relationship. In contrast, if one of the friends always gives and the other always receives, the relationship can become unbalanced, which can lead to resentment or dependency.

This concept also applies to other areas of life, such as work. In the professional realm, giving can mean putting in extra time to help a coworker, sharing knowledge, or taking on additional responsibilities. However, if we are always giving without receiving recognition, support, or respite, we can burn out. It is important to know when it is time to ask for help or accept collaboration from others. Otherwise, we can end up feeling overburdened and exhausted, which will eventually affect our ability to continue giving effectively.

The balance between giving and receiving also has implications for our personal lives. If we are constantly giving in our relationships, whether with family, friends or partners, without allowing ourselves to receive, we are likely to end up feeling drained or neglected. Giving all the time without receiving anything in return can lead to emotional imbalance. Feeling like our needs are not being met can lead to frustration or even resentment. Therefore, it is essential that we cultivate relationships where there is a mutual flow of support, where both giving and receiving are a natural part of the interaction.

Furthermore, it is important to understand that the act of receiving is not only about material or tangible things. Sometimes receiving means accepting words of encouragement, tokens of affection, or even someone's time and attention. Appreciating these small gestures is part of the process of keeping ourselves balanced. Not everything we give or receive has to be something big or significant in appearance; what really matters is the spirit in which it is done.

It's also critical to remember that giving and receiving isn't just about our interactions with others, but also how we treat ourselves. Giving doesn't always mean sacrificing ourselves for others; it can also mean giving ourselves the time and space to take care of ourselves.

Likewise, receiving doesn't always mean accepting help from others, but also being responsive to our own needs. This includes things like taking time off when we need it, taking time to relax, or doing something we enjoy. The balance between giving and receiving starts with ourselves.

Finally, learning to balance giving and receiving is not something that happens overnight. It is a process that requires practice, self-reflection, and sometimes adjustments in the way we interact with others and ourselves. There is no exact formula, but the key is to be aware of our needs and limits, both in giving and receiving. When we achieve this balance, we feel more satisfied, less stressed, and more in tune with the natural flow of life.

In short, the balance between giving and receiving is an essential part of a harmonious life. Both are necessary for our well-being and for maintaining healthy, meaningful relationships. By learning to give generously and receive gratefully, we create a positive cycle that nourishes ourselves and others, allowing us to live more fulfilled and balanced lives.

A Daily Practice

A daily practice is essential to maintaining balance in life, because it allows us to create habits that anchor us, give us structure, and help us face everyday challenges in a calmer, more focused way. It's not about doing extraordinary things or following rigid routines. Rather, it's about finding small actions that we can do every day, that help us stay in tune with ourselves and the world around us. These actions, when they become part of our daily lives, can make a huge difference to our mental, physical, and emotional health.

The first step in establishing a daily practice is to identify what your most immediate needs are. This can vary from person to person. Some people may need a practice that helps them feel calmer, while others may be looking for a routine that motivates and energizes them. The important thing is that the daily practice you choose makes sense for you and fits into your life and circumstances. It doesn't have to be complicated or time-consuming; in fact, the most effective practices are often the simplest.

An effective daily practice can start with something as basic as taking a few minutes each morning to breathe deeply. Mindful breathing is a simple yet powerful technique that helps us connect with the present, calm our minds, and reduce stress. When you become aware of your breathing, you give yourself space to stop and recharge, which can be very helpful before starting a busy day. You only need to take a few minutes to close your eyes, inhale deeply through your nose, exhale slowly through your mouth, and repeat this several times. Although it may seem like a small gesture, starting your day in this way can completely change your mood and disposition.

Another daily practice that many people find helpful is intention setting. Each morning, before you dive into your tasks, you can take a moment to think about what you'd like to accomplish that day. It doesn't have to be a big or ambitious goal; in fact, it can be something as simple as "I want to be more present today" or "I want to take better care of my health today." Setting intentions helps us stay focused on what really matters and reminds us of the purpose behind our daily actions. Throughout the day, you can return to that intention whenever you feel yourself getting off track or losing balance.

Self-care is also a crucial part of any daily practice. We live in a world that constantly pushes us to do more, to be more productive, and we often forget to take care of ourselves. Incorporating small moments of self-care into your daily routine can help you maintain balance and avoid burnout. This can mean dedicating a few minutes to an activity you enjoy, such as reading a good book, listening to your favorite music, or going for a walk. Don't underestimate the power of these moments. Often, what we need to feel better are not big changes, but small breaks that allow us to disconnect from stress and reconnect with ourselves.

Physical exercise is another daily practice that can greatly contribute to your overall balance. You don't have to do intense workouts or spend hours at the gym to notice the benefits. A little bit of movement every day is enough to improve your physical and mental health. You can start with something as simple as walking for 20 minutes, doing gentle stretches, or practicing yoga. Movement not only helps you keep your body active, but it also releases endorphins, which are the hormones that make us feel good.

This type of daily practice will not only help you stay fit, but it will also give you more energy and help you clear your mind.

It's also helpful to incorporate gratitude into your daily practice. Taking a moment each day to reflect on the things you're grateful for can completely change your perspective. Often, we focus so much on what we don't have or what we're worried about that we forget to appreciate what we do have. Gratitude helps us stay centered and remember that even if things aren't perfect, there's always something good in our lives. You can do this at the end of the day by journaling three things you're grateful for, or by simply taking a minute to think about them before you go to sleep. It's a small but very powerful habit that will help you end your day on a positive note.

Another essential component of a balanced daily practice is learning to unplug. We live in an age where technology dominates much of our lives, and while it has many benefits, it can also be a constant source of stress and distraction. Setting aside time each day to disconnect from your phone, television, and other screens is vital to maintaining a healthy mental state. You can set aside a time of day, such as dinnertime or right before bed, to be technology-free and allow yourself to enjoy the present moment without interruption. This simple practice can do wonders for your mental well-being.

Mindful eating can also be part of your daily practice. Often, we eat automatically, without paying attention to what we're eating or how it makes us feel. Taking time to enjoy each bite, savoring your food, and being present during meals can help you have a healthier relationship with food. Not only does this benefit your physical health, it also allows you to enjoy the experience of eating more, which is an important part of self-care.

Finally, consistency is key when it comes to a daily practice. It's not about being perfect or following a strict routine every day without exception. There will be days when you feel more motivated and other days when things don't go as planned, and that's okay. The important thing is that over time, the small actions you take on a daily basis add up and start to have a positive impact on your life. Don't beat yourself up if you can't do everything you set out to do one day; instead, try again the next day. The key is persistence and staying committed to your own well-being.

In short, a daily practice is a simple and effective way to maintain balance amidst the demands and distractions of modern life. Whether you choose to spend a few minutes doing conscious breathing, set intentions for the day, practice gratitude, get moving, or unplug from technology, the important thing is that these small actions become habits. Over time, these practices will help you feel more centered, balanced, and at peace with yourself, allowing you to face life's challenges with greater clarity and calm.